Gay

Everything You Need to Know About

SEXUAL ABSTINENCE

All couples are faced with the decision of whether or not to have sex. Consider all the options, including abstaining from sex until marriage, before making your decision.

Everything You Need to Know About

SEXUAL ABSTINENCE

Barbara Moe

THE ROSEN PUBLISHING GROUP, INC.
NEW YORK

Published in 1996 by The Rosen Publishing Group, Inc.
29 East 21st Street, New York, NY 10010

Copyright 1996 by The Rosen Publishing Group, Inc.

First Edition

Manufactured in the United States of America

Library of Congress Cataloging-in-Publication Data

Moe, Barbara A.
    Everything you need to know about sexual abstinence / Barbara Moe. —
1st ed.
      p.   cm. — (The need to know library)
    Includes bibliographical references and index.
    Summary: Presents facts about human sexuality and discusses the
choices teenagers face in deciding whether or not to be sexually
active.
    ISBN 0-8239-2104-2
    1. Teenagers—United States—Sexual behavior—Juvenile literature.
2. Sexual abstinence—United States—Juvenile literature. 3. Sex
instruction for youth—United States—Juvenile literature.
4. Sexual ethics—United States—Juvenile literature. [1. Sexual
ethics. 2. Sex instruction for youth. 3. Youth sexual behavior.]
I. Title. II. Series.
HQ27.M62   1995
613.9′07—dc20   95-21957
                                                        CIP
                                                         AC

Contents

1. What's This All About?   7

2. Your Body   14

3. What Is Sexual Abstinence?   22

4. Why Choose Sexual Abstinence?   36

5. How to Say No   47

Glossary—*Explaining New Words*   57

Where to Get Help   60

For Further Reading   62

Index   63

Every day you are confronted with sexual images of some sort, whether it is on television, in the movies, or in advertisements.

Chapter 1

What's This All About?

"*Sex? It's out there all right. Everywhere. Just like the air we breathe," says Bob. "Turn around. What do you see? Half-naked bodies. TV, movies, billboards. Close your eyes and put on your headphones. What do you hear? Song lyrics about sex. 'Do it! It's fun.' 'Don't do it. It's dangerous.' I don't know what to think."*

Bob is right. Sexual choices are confusing. So are many of the other life choices you have to make. But the good news is that you *can* choose. You don't have to do anything you don't want to do. This book presents facts to help with your choices.

"I can't honestly say sex is all I think about," Bob continues. "There's sports and food. And I worry about violence and dying. My friends talk a lot about girls. I mostly listen. I don't believe everything they say. I've never even kissed a girl,

except my mom. To tell you the truth, I'm a little scared of girls. I'm not certain how to act around them."

You Are a Sexual Person

You are a sexual person. Everyone is, from newborn babies to the elderly. Being sexual isn't something you have to *do*. Being sexual is something you already *are*.

Your body is equipped with *sex organs*. Sex organs are the parts of your body that are involved with *reproduction*, or the ability to have a baby. When you are a teenager, your body produces *hormones*. Hormones are chemicals that cause your sexual organs to mature. The physical changes that occur when you are a teenager affect how you feel about yourself and others. For many teens, adjusting to the changes is awkward. You may think sexual thoughts more than ever. You may feel uncomfortable about your appearance. Like Bob, you may be nervous about relationships. You may have questions about your thoughts and feelings.

This is normal. Your body is undergoing a big change, and it takes time to get used to it. Your body may be ready to have sex, but that does not mean that you are. Perhaps you want to wait to have sex until your thoughts and feelings catch up with your body. That is a wise choice. Be patient with yourself. You do not have to do something sexual until *you* feel comfortable about doing it.

It's Normal. Okay?

Sexual thoughts and feelings are normal. Almost everyone has them. Even old people. And most little kids (if you can remember) are curious about their sexual parts. As a teenager, your sexual impulses get stronger. You may:

- have dreams, thoughts, and feelings about sexual things. For example, Anna idolized her female camp counselor and began to ask herself, "Am I gay?"
- feel like "making out" with your boyfriend or girlfriend
- want to touch yourself in a sexual way.

These impulses are normal. Part of becoming an adult is learning to deal with these sexual feelings in a healthy way.

Decisions, Decisions

Having sex is different from having sexual feelings. Being sexually active is one way to express sexual feelings. It is not the only way, and it is not necessarily the best way. No matter what anyone else tells you about how "everyone is doing it," you are the one who must decide whether and when *you* want to become sexually active.

Should you be sexually active? Learn the facts. Then decide for yourself. Many teenagers don't know the facts. Most do not plan their first sexual intercourse. They just let it happen, and many times they are not prepared. But a girl can get pregnant the *first time* she has sex. In addition, it is easy to contract a sexually transmitted disease (STD) if a condom, a rubber sheath that covers the penis, is not used. AIDS (acquired immuno-deficiency syndrome) is the most serious of all STDS. There is currently no cure for AIDS; it is always fatal.

This book discusses sex and provides information that will help you be in control of your own sexual choices.

What Are the Facts?

Here are a few to start with:

- One out of every four babies is born to an unmarried teen.
- One in seven young people will get a sexually transmitted disease.
- The number of cases of AIDS is doubling every year in people under the age of 20.

Choices

Having sex is a voluntary choice, like whether you will go to a particular movie. But when you have sex, much more is at stake.

Some people forget the choice part. They let friends or the media tell them that "everybody's doing it." They ask themselves, "If I don't do it, am I abnormal? Do I have to have sex to be a 'real' man? Do I have to have sex to be a 'real' woman?" The answer to all these questions is no.

You may be feeling pressure to become sexually active, but it is important to listen to yourself. Ask yourself honestly: Do you want to become sexually active? If you do, is it because that's what *you* want? Or do you want to become sexually active to please *other* people, such as a boyfriend or girlfriend, or to fit in? These are understandable reasons. But more important is how you feel about yourself. Listen to yourself. If you choose not to be sexually active, that is fine. You are not abnormal; you are taking care of yourself. And if you choose to become sexually active, protect yourself. But remember: It is *your* choice.

Myth: If you don't use your sexual body parts, they will get rusty and stop working.

Fact: If you don't use the sexual parts of your body, they'll wait. They will remain in excellent condition until the day you are ready to use them.

Myth: A person needs sex to be "fulfilled."

Fact: Many things fulfill a person. Sex can be

Life consists of a series of decisions. Some, such as which cereal to eat for breakfast, are easy. Others, such as whether or not to have sex, are more difficult and require much more consideration.

one of them, but it doesn't have to be. Fulfillment often comes from a good relationship with another person. Fulfillment is more mental than physical. Sex *can* be part of a relationship, but it doesn't *have* to be.

Suppose you are dating someone. If he or she insists on having sex in order to be fulfilled and you are uncomfortable about that idea, you have a right to express your feelings. Respect yourself.

One Choice

Based on the facts, sexual abstinence until marriage (not having sex until you marry) is a choice many young people are making. Some people believe it is the best choice.

Chapter 2

Your Body

Knowing about your body and how it functions will help you make responsible decisions about sex. The following sections describe your sexual organs and the way your body is affected by puberty.

Males

The main male sex organs (genitals) are the penis and the scrotum. The testicles (balls) are inside the scrotum. Males produce sperm in their testicles. During sex, the male penis gets hard (erect). The time of greatest sexual excitement is called orgasm. When a man and woman are having sexual intercourse and the male has an orgasm, sperm comes through his penis into the woman's vagina. This can cause pregnancy.

OUTER FEMALE SEXUAL ORGANS

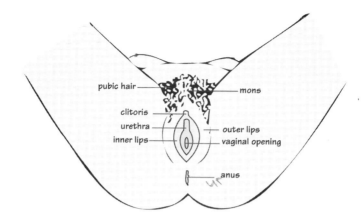

pubic hair — — mons

clitoris —
urethra —
inner lips — — outer lips
— vaginal opening

— anus

INNER FEMALE SEXUAL ORGANS

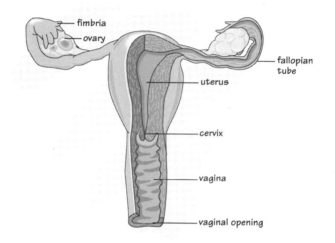

— fimbria
— ovary

fallopian
tube

uterus

cervix

vagina

vaginal opening

MALE SEXUAL ORGANS

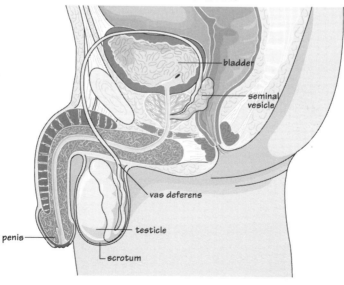

bladder

seminal
vesicle

vas deferens

penis —

testicle

scrotum

Females

Girls have sexual organs inside and outside their bodies. Therefore, they are sometimes less aware of what their sexual organs look like. If you want to get a more accurate picture, squat over a mirror and use a flashlight. Knowing about your body isn't shameful. It's smart.

Outside. The outside area between a girl's legs is called the genital area or vulva. A girl or woman has "lips" in the genital area. The outer or large lips (labia) are the labia majora. Inside the large lips are small lips (labia minora). The clitoris is a little bud at the top of the small lips. It is very sensitive. Stimulation of the clitoris gives women sexual pleasure. When a woman is sexually aroused, the blood vessels in her genital area, clitoris, and inner lips swell, and her clitoris becomes erect. When she has an orgasm, tension is released in a series of muscle contractions.

Inside. The inside organs are the vagina, uterus, fallopian tubes, and ovaries. The uterus is the pear-shaped organ that expands to let a baby grow inside. The vagina is the flexible tubelike structure that stretches to let the baby pass through from the uterus to the world. Blood flows out through the vagina during menstrual periods. The fallopian tubes extend from the top of the uterus to the ovaries, where eggs are stored.

If an egg and a sperm meet, pregnancy results.

What's Happening?

You probably know about puberty. Puberty begins and ends sometime between ages 8 and 16. During puberty hormones come on strong. Hormones cause sexual growth and changes in your sexual organs. They also increase your desire to have sex.

What Are the Body's Changes?

Sexual maturing is a slow process. Sometimes a "growth spurt" *seems* to have happened overnight: But in fact, the whole process of puberty takes from two years to six years. During this time, you can adjust to your body's changes.

Girls

One of the first things girls notice in puberty is breast growth. (Boys' breasts sometimes start to develop too, but this growth is only temporary.) Some girls worry that their breasts are too big. Others think their breasts are too small. But whatever size a young woman's breasts are, they will be able to carry out the job of making milk for a baby if the woman becomes pregnant.

During puberty, girls get more fat around their hips, upper legs, and buttocks. They may also have increased secretions (wetness) in their vaginal area.

Next, menstrual periods begin. Once a month

Getting her period is only one of the steps a young woman takes on the road to becoming an adult.

the lining of the uterus (womb) sheds (falls away). This is called menstruation. Some people call menstruation "the curse," but it is a healthy sign of womanhood. One thing some young women (and some young men) don't understand: Once a girl starts having periods, she can get pregnant—even if she's only 12 or 13.

Here are some other facts you need to know:

- Girls can get pregnant even when they're having their period.
- Girls can get pregnant even when using birth control.
- Girls can get pregnant even if a boy withdraws his penis before he has ejaculated.

- Girls can get pregnant even if they have sex standing up.
- Girls can get pregnant after they've had an abortion.
- Girls can get pregnant even when they're breast-feeding.
- Girls can get pregnant even if they douche (rinse out their vagina) after intercourse.
- Girls can get pregnant even when they don't want to.

"I got pregnant at fifteen. I knew I was too young to raise a kid. But my mom talked me into keeping him. By the time he was four, neither one of us could control him. We had to take him to social services. I will never stop feeling terrible about that."

One sure way *not* to get pregnant is *not* to have sexual intercourse. This is known as practicing abstinence.

Boys

Sexual changes and growth spurts in young men start a bit later. That's why eighth-grade girls sometimes look so large compared to eighth-grade boys. Between the ages of 12 and 16, the male sex organs (penis and scrotum) begin to grow. Male hormones cause increased sperm production. The testicles make sperm. During sex, the penis releases sperm in a liquid called semen. If a sperm

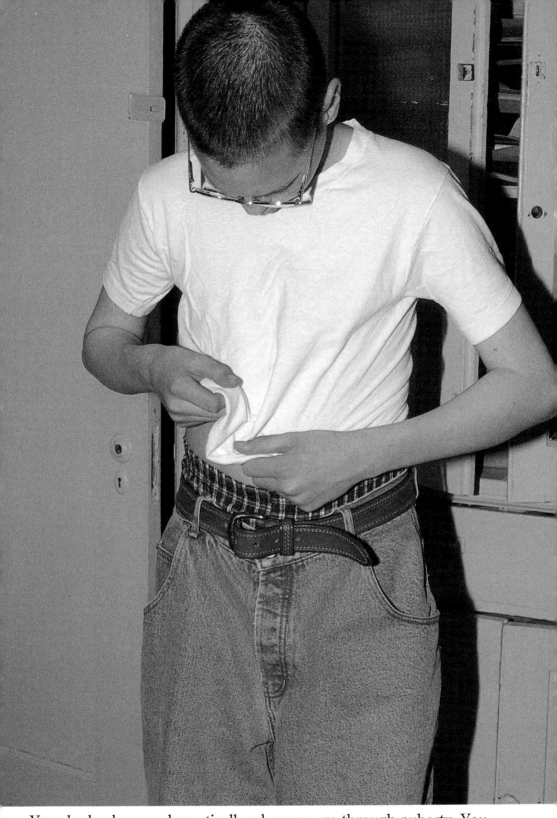

Your body changes dramatically when you go through puberty. You may find that you grow out of your clothes very quickly.

reaches an egg in the female, pregnancy can result.

Also, teenage males may have "wet dreams." At night a reflex erection causes the release of sperm. These "nocturnal emissions," as they are sometimes called, cause unexpected wetness. Like girls' menstrual periods, this can be embarrassing. So can uncontrolled erections of the penis. But these reflexes are normal signs of growing up.

During puberty, boys' voices also become lower, and they grow hair on their faces.

Common Changes

During the teen years, both males and females experience:

- growth of the sex organs
- acne (pimples)
- oily skin and hair
- growth of body hair under the arms, in the pubic area (around sexual organs), and on the legs
- smelly sweat (body odor or B.O.).

Males and females have a lot in common. In the teenage years, everyone is going through physical and emotional changes. The end result is a mature person. Before that time comes, each person has to make some hard decisions.

Chapter 3

What Is Sexual Abstinence?

Before you define "sexual abstinence," you have to define what "having sex" means. You may be thinking, "C 'mon, *everyone* knows what having sex means." But people get into arguments about the meaning of "sex." (You may have heard other terms, such as "doing it," "screwing," or "going all the way.")

People disagree about the meaning of both abstinence and sex. Abstinence comes from "abstain," which means to "stay away from." You can choose to abstain from a lot of things—alcohol, drugs, cigarettes, meat, candy. When you abstain from these things, you don't use them. (Other terms used to describe sexual abstinence are "celibacy" and "chastity.")

Sexual abstinence means postponing sexual intercourse, usually until marriage. If you decide abstinence is for you, then you will *not* "go all the way." You may believe, however, that kissing, necking, and petting are okay. In other words, "making out" is fine with you. For you, as long as you're not having sexual intercourse, you're okay.

People who believe in abstinence may be separated into two camps. Let's call them the Touchers (Hands-on People) and the Non-Touchers (Hands-off People).

Tyler

"I'm not having any more hands-on stuff until I get married. That will probably be when I'm about forty! I had a bad experience with a girl I really liked. She'd signed one of those abstinence pledge cards. But on this hot summer night at the beach she said she wanted a back rub. One thing led to another. We both got carried away. You know what I mean. After that night, she said she never wanted to see me again, and she hasn't."

Tyler believes that kissing in a sexual way, petting, and necking can be lead-ins to the real thing. Tyler is a Non-Toucher. He says that if people practice true abstinence, they avoid "getting physical." If two people get started, argue the Non-Touchers, one or both parties may not want, or be able, to stop. They will eventually let their urges "carry them away." They will battle temptation, but temptation may win.

Some people believe that some sexual activity such as kissing can substitute for sexual intercourse.

Amy

"Tyler's view is absolutely ridiculous! You can't tell me that a girl and a guy are going to go with each other for a long time and never touch. What are we supposed to do when we go out? Sit on our hands?"

Touchers, such as Amy, agree that sexual urges are strong. But they think passionate kisses, necking, and petting can be *substitutes* for sexual intercourse. After all, the Touchers argue, you don't get a disease from *touching* someone. A couple can express romantic feelings by kissing and touching without "going all the way."

Rosemary

"I don't see anything wrong with kissing, but nobody's getting me *undressed in the back seat of a car. As you can see, I have strong feelings on this subject. No sex until marriage. I don't want to get* AIDS *or get pregnant. I don't have time for a kid right now. Don't get me wrong. I'm no prude. My boyfriend and I kiss and hug. But there's a definite line we don't cross. It's just there. He knows it and I know it."*

Rosemary has a middle-of-the-road viewpoint. She believes that she and her boyfriend can touch each other to a certain extent, but she doesn't think that everything except intercourse is okay.

You must decide for yourself what abstinence means. It's a good idea to discuss the matter with your partner, so you're both on the same wavelength.

Love and Sex

Abstinence means waiting to have sex until you're sure you are ready for all the responsibilities that go with a long-term, committed, loving relationship, usually marriage.

Responsibilities! What responsibilities? you might be wondering. For instance, being loyal to your partner; being willing to compromise; standing by your partner, even when it is difficult, and working things out together; being

Loving someone does not mean you have to have sex with the person.

trustworthy; being honest about your feelings; keeping your promises; taking mutual responsibility for practicing safer sex. Love is more than a feeling. Love is the glue that keeps people together in good times and bad.

Love is a hard word to define. It's a short word, and yet it has a big meaning. When you see your partner, your heart races and your body feels like a wet dish rag. But love is more than this heart-thumping. Love matures and deepens as a relationship matures.

Loving is caring for another person as much as you care about yourself. The crazy thing is that you have to love yourself before you can really love another person. Another word for self-love is *self-esteem*. The next chapter talks more about self-esteem and how you can develop it.

Some Common Questions About Love and Sex

Question: How can I tell if I'm really in love?

Answer: That is a difficult question, but part of the answer involves time. See how long this feeling lasts. If your love (or your partner's love) wears down in a couple of months, it was not really love. It was probably infatuation. If you're in doubt about your love for another person, here are some questions to ask yourself.

- As time goes on, am I finding more and more things to like about my partner?
- Is my partner a good friend (or just a sexual interest)? Do we talk well together?
- Do my partner and I trust each other without a doubt? Are lying and cheating out of the question?
- Are the challenges we face together as a couple making our love stronger?
- Does my partner treat me as an equal?

Question: I've always thought sex was one of the most important parts of a love relationship. Are you saying it's not?

Answer: Sometimes people think they want *sex*

but what they are really searching for is *emotional intimacy.* Intimacy is letting your emotional walls down and allowing another person to get close to you. When we say emotionally close, we don't mean two sweaty bodies breathing hard. Emotional intimacy is letting another person know your deepest thoughts and fears. What scares you the most? What do you want to do with your life? What are your hurts? Having sex can be a *part* of emotional intimacy. But sex is not necessary for two people to have real intimacy. In fact, some people use sexual acts to *avoid* emotional intimacy.

Question: How do people use sex to avoid emotional intimacy?

Answer: Some people are not comfortable talking about their emotions. Often without realizing it, they substitute the good feeling of having sex (physical intimacy) for the good feeling of emotional intimacy. They are letting someone get physically close to them but are guarding their emotions. They are usually afraid that if they reveal themselves—their deepest secrets, their darkest fears—their partner will reject them.

But if two people do reveal themselves emotionally, they might like each other that much more. Some people have said that abstinence makes the heart grow fonder. This is because a relationship between two people who agree to be abstinent is based more on emotional than physical intimacy.

It can be difficult to share your feelings with your partner, but sharing is an important aspect of a good relationship.

Question: How do love and sex go together? I know they're not the same, but . . .

Answer: You're right. Love and sex are not the same. Sex can be a wonderful part of a committed relationship. Sex can express love. But sex that is not based on love can create problems. Some people decide to have sex before they're ready and later feel that they've let themselves down. Others don't *decide* anything; they just have sex without any preparation. This can be *very* risky. Others may love each other, but one or both may feel that they are not yet ready for the responsibility of a sexual relationship. If one person feels unready, the other person should respect those wishes.

Question: What's the big deal about people having sex when they're not ready?

Answer: There are physical and emotional consequences to having sex, whether a person is ready to have sex or not. First, even if birth control is used, a girl can get pregnant. If that happens, the father and mother must face the question: Are we prepared to make the commitment to raising a child? Second, a person can contract AIDS (for which there is as yet no cure) or another STD from someone who is already infected. (That other person may infect someone else without even knowing that he or she is infected.)

Persons who were ready for sex would have a difficult time with either of these consequences. Persons who *were not* ready for sex (who had allowed themselves to be talked into it or who felt they "ought" to have sex) will have the same difficulties *and* may feel guilty, resentful, and angry at themselves.

In addition, sex changes a relationship. It intensifies a relationship and excludes other people, sometimes resulting in a loss of friends. Emotional pressure builds in the relationship. Sex sometimes becomes expected. Jealousy can become intense. Feelings get hurt.

If you are not comfortable or willing to take on these physical and emotional consequences, don't be afraid to say how you feel. No one has the right to push you into something you're not ready for.

Question: Isn't sex supposed to be wonderful?

Answer: In a long-term committed love relationship, sex can be a wonderful experience. But the sexual realities of many young people aren't so great. Many young men think of themselves and their desires and not their partner's. Young women, expecting ecstasy, often feel instead nothing or even discomfort.

Question: How are you going to know how to do all that sexual stuff when you're married if you don't try it out beforehand? And how will you know if you're sexually compatible with someone you might want to marry?

Answer: Don't worry. You *will* figure it out. You will also find that there are many ways to express physical intimacy. You don't have to be a sexual athlete when you get married. Sex is more meaningful as part of a committed relationship.

Not everyone is doing it—having sex, that is. In fact, nearly half of American teenagers are *not.*

Some Common Questions About Homosexuality

Question: I'm a 16-year-old girl. The problem is I feel attracted to my female P. E. teacher. I think about her a lot. I get all nervous and silly when she talks to me. Do you think I'm gay?

Answer: Almost everyone at one time or another has felt a strong attraction to a person of the same sex. It's normal. Maybe it's a teacher, a coach, or a camp counselor. It doesn't necessarily mean that you're gay.

Question: What does being "gay" mean? Is that when men dress up in women's clothes?

Answer: "Gay" is another word for *homosexual.* People who are homosexual (sexually attracted to those of the same sex) may be born that way. *Bisexuals* are people attracted to both males and females. *Lesbians* are women sexually attracted to other women. *Heterosexuals* are people attracted to the opposite sex.

A person who dresses up in clothing of the opposite sex is called a *transvestite* or *cross-dresser.* Very few homosexuals do this.

Question: Can too-strict mothers make their sons gay?

Answer: No one *makes* someone else gay. You can't make yourself gay either.

Question: I've heard stories about child-molesting homosexuals. Are they true?

Answer: Homosexuals are no more likely to abuse someone than heterosexuals. In fact, most child molesters are heterosexual.

Question: How many people are gay?

Answer: About 10 percent of males and 3 percent of females.

Almost everyone has sexual feelings. Some homosexuals have high self-esteem and are comfortable with themselves. Others feel terrible—guilty, worried, seeing themselves as abnormal, uncomfortable about their sexuality.

Wally

"I knew this kid at school, James. He was really smart and seemed to have no problems. He had a mother, a father, a sister, a brother. One big happy family. He had a lot of friends. But one day he went home, got out his father's gun, and shot himself in the head. He left a note that said, 'It wasn't your fault.' His family's really broken up about it. One of his friends think it happened because James was having a hard time dealing with the fact that he was homosexual."

What a tragedy—if James was homosexual and thought his only option was suicide. Because homosexuals are a minority, it may be hard for a homosexual teen to find someone who relates to his or her situation. But support is there.

If you or someone you know is gay, there are people to talk to. A counselor, a support group, or a gay and lesbian community center will help. You will learn (as anyone should) to:

- be aware of your sexual feelings
- accept your sexual feelings and yourself as a sexual person with these feelings
- choose whether or not you want to act on your sexual feelings.

For gay and lesbian teens, too, abstinence is an important option. Why? Sex changes a homosexual relationship in the same way that it changes a heterosexual relationship. The relationship becomes more intense.

In addition, you can still get sexually transmitted diseases. You can still get AIDS, especially if you have anal intercourse.

Remember that sexual preferences (likes and dislikes) are a person's own business. Sexual practices (what a person does sexually) are also up to each person. You can make *your* own choices. Don't let anyone else pressure you. Be comfortable with your own sexual feelings and decisions.

Whatever your sexual preference, consider abstinence.

Who's for Abstinence?

Starting a few years ago, various organizations began pushing for abstinence. One of these groups is Athletes for Abstinence (AFA), a division of the A. C. Green Programs for Youth. This group promotes sexual purity until marriage. AFA has made a video endorsing abstinence called *It Ain't Worth It*. The musical documentary stars A. C. Green of the Phoenix Suns, David Robinson of the San Antonio Spurs, and Darrell Green of the Washington Redskins.

Even people who have had sex one or more

times are joining in. It is never too late to start being abstinent.

Choices

Life is full of choices. With sex, you have one of three choices.

One choice is to go ahead and have sex without much knowledge or preparation. Then you will have to live with the possible consequences—pregnancy, AIDS, other sexually transmitted disease. And you may hurt yourself emotionally.

The second is to learn about your body before you have sex. Think hard about what you're doing and why. Consider how you feel. Take precautions but know the precautions aren't foolproof. (You still have to live with the possible consequences.)

The third choice, for those who do not want to be faced with the possible consequences of sex, is abstinence.

Chapter 4

Why Choose Sexual Abstinence?

Abstinence means making the choice to delay sexual intercourse until marriage. It is the only sure way to avoid pregnancy and sexually transmitted diseases. Abstinence is based on *respect* and *responsibility*.

The Two Rs

If you care about someone, you respect that person. You want the best for him or her, and that requires responsibility. Respect and responsibility involve taking care of:

Yourself. If you think caring for yourself is selfish, think again. The ability to respect *yourself* is the basis of all healthy relationships. Every morning you look in the mirror. You face yourself. Do you like what you see? If not, why not? Remember: You are unique, one of a kind. Sooner

The choice of whether or not to have sex is yours to make, but you will have to live with the consequences of your decision for the rest of your life.

or later you will move out of your parents' home. You may move in with someone else. But you will always have to live with yourself.

Think about the sexual decisions you will have to make. Will you decide to do what's best for you? In the short term? In the long run? Do you have moral or religious beliefs about premarital sex? If you act against these beliefs, how will you feel?

Here's another thing to remember. You can choose whether you want to have sex or not. It's your decision, your body, your life. Are you considering premarital sex mainly to feel more grown up? Are you being honest with the most important person in your life, yourself? Don't expect someone *else* to make you happy. Make yourself happy. Show respect for your body and your emotions. Take care of them. Take responsibility for your own decisions.

Your partner. It doesn't matter if you're male or female. Show respect for the other person.

Do:

- Communicate. Be honest. Say directly what you think and feel. Get your emotions out in the open.
- Consider the consequences of your actions. How will your actions affect the other person?

Don't:

- Force sex on someone who doesn't want it.
- Even *think* about having sex with someone if you think you might get a sexually transmitted disease.

Ask yourself these questions:

- Am I feeling pressured to have sex?
- What are my true feelings about this person?
- Are my partner and I able to communicate?
- How does each of us feel about different things?

Your Children. "Children? I don't have any." But you might if you choose to have sex before

You and your partner must talk honestly about how you each feel about having sex. You both have a stake in your decision.

marriage. Maybe you've already had sex and a child didn't result. There's always a first time. Emily says, "He told me he was sterile, and I believed him. Now I'm six months pregnant." Having sex is serious business. Bringing a child into the world will change your life *forever*. A child isn't like a puppy. You can't return it. You can't assume that another member of your family will agree to raise it.

Your Friends and Family. To be abstinent or not is your decision. But your decision will affect your friends and your family. What if you decide to become sexually active against your parents' wishes? What if your parents find out? Can you accept the fall-out? What if you get a sexually transmitted disease and have to go to your parents for help? What if a pregnancy results?

"I was thirteen when my sister got pregnant. She was fifteen. The whole thing ruined my life. She didn't even know who the father was. The guys in my class expected me to be just like her, which I'm not. My little niece is cute and I love her. But my parents are crabby all the time. They're tired of baby-sitting and having a kid around. So am I."

Sexually Transmitted Disease (STD)

"I met this guy at an amusement park. He worked there. He was so handsome and tan, a real hunk. I smiled at him, and he smiled back. He asked me to meet him after his shift. He was older and had his own apartment. We went over there and, well . . . Not too long after that, I got real sick with a headache and fever. I thought it was just the flu. Then my crotch started itching, then hurting like crazy. My mom took me to a doctor, and they both grilled me. I found out I had herpes. It was humiliating and still is."

Sexually transmitted diseases are sometimes called STDs. The old term was venereal disease or VD. The desire not to contract sexually transmitted

Knowing the risks involved in entering a sexual relationship may help you make your decision.

diseases is one of the main reasons why many young people today are choosing abstinence.

All sexually transmitted diseases are very contagious. Having sexual intercourse even once with someone who is infected can expose a person to AIDS or another STD. There are at least twenty STDS. They can cause:

- infertility (difficulty getting pregnant or getting a partner pregnant)
- sterility (total inability to have children throughout your lifetime)
- diseases of the central nervous system
- abdominal and genital pain
- death.

Some sexually transmitted diseases can be treated. But telling parents and seeing a doctor can be embarrassing. AIDS is a fatal disease. It has no cure. If you think ahead to these possible consequences, you too may decide on abstinence.

AIDS

AIDS is the most dangerous sexually transmitted disease of today. It is always fatal. The small virus (HIV—human immunodeficiency virus) that may cause AIDS lives quietly in the infected person's body cells. Sometimes years go by before the person begins to feel sick. During that time, the person can pass on the virus (by sexual intercourse) to someone else. People who have contracted the HIV in their teens may feel well for years. Then one day, they begin to get sick. The virus destroys the immune system (the part of the body that fights off disease).

It is estimated by the federal Centers for Disease Control and Prevention that at least one million people in the United States are already infected with HIV. The bad news is that there is no cure. Pregnant women can pass the disease to their unborn babies. Some of these babies die. The good news is that you can keep yourself from getting AIDS. Not having sexual intercourse is the best prevention. (You can have *safer* sex by using condoms with anti-HIV spermicides, but you are never guaranteed to have totally safe sex.)

Some of the other sexually transmitted diseases are herpes, chlamydia, syphilis, and gonorrhea.

Pregnancy

Teen pregnancy is no party. The threat of an unwanted pregnancy is another good reason for abstinence. Many unmarried young men and women think they want a baby. However, almost every single teen parent eventually has second thoughts. Think ahead a few years. Do you want to be dragging a four-year-old to preschool when you haven't even finished high school yourself? If you're not pregnant now or haven't gotten someone pregnant, be grateful for your good sense (or good luck). Here are some reasons that your choice is a smart one:

- Being a teen mother is one sure way to be poor.
- Getting married and "living happily ever after" may not happen. Half of married young people get divorced in five years.
- Being a teen mother or father forces you to take on extra responsibilities at a time of life that is already difficult.
- Teen pregnancy is one reason boys, as well as girls, drop out of school.
- Babies born to young mothers have more birth defects than other babies.
- Teen mothers have more complicated (difficult) pregnancies.
- Getting pregnant and keeping the baby affects your whole family.

Over their lifetimes, teen mothers earn roughly half the income of women who wait until their twenties to have children. Of all women currently on welfare, more than half had their first child when they were teenagers. More than 40,000 pregnant teens drop out of school every year. And in 1991, 69 percent of the teen mothers who gave birth were unmarried.

Choosing Abstinence

Young people decide to be sexually abstinent for other reasons as well. Some don't want to get a reputation for being "easy." For others, having sex may ruin an otherwise good relationship. It may also make breaking up harder.

Other teens are worried about getting caught. Carl says, "We were making out in her family room, and her mom came home early from work. She had a migraine headache, but after she caught us, I was the one with the headache!"

If you are considering abstinence, here are some important *don'ts.*

- Don't be ignorant about how girls get pregnant and about how to prevent it. And even if you don't plan to be sexually active, learn about AIDS and other sexually transmitted diseases. *Why* is the safest sex no sex? If you know the facts, you can tell others.
- Don't drink. Alcohol interferes with your ability to make smart decisions and with your willpower.
- Don't be afraid to talk to your date about your sexual attitudes. Communicate. Try to find out his or her views *before* things get physical.
- Don't rely only on a person's looks. Looks can be deceiving. Instead, listen to your instincts. If you find yourself in an uncomfortable situation, get out of it. This will help you keep out of dangerous situations, such as date rape.

So Why Do Some People Do It Anyway?

With all the reasons *not* to have sex, why do some teens do it anyway?

- To get back at their parents.
- To find out what it's like.
- To "get it over with."
- Because they're high (under the influence of alcohol and/or drugs).
- To make someone else jealous.
- To try to get him or her to love them.
- To try to get the other person tied to them. ("If I have his baby, I'll still have a part of him.")
- To prove something. ("I've had sex, so I must be grown-up.")
- To feel sexual. (But remember that you already are a sexual person.)
- Because they were pressured.

As you can see, some of these reasons for having sex do not make sense. Think things over ahead of time. Then you will be more likely to think straight when the pressure is on you to make a decision about sex. Abstinence is based upon respect—for yourself and others. Postponing sex is one way of taking responsibility for your life and the lives of others. If you consider the potential lifelong effects of having sex (AIDS, other sexually transmitted disease, unplanned and unwanted pregnancy), abstinence is a good choice.

Chapter 5

How to Say No

*"G*rown-ups don't understand peer pressure," says Morgan. "Abstinence is easy for them to say. Abstinence sounds like a great idea, but I want to know how we're supposed to do it."

Many young people say they would choose abstinence, but they need help in saying no. They want to be accepted. They want to be careful not to hurt another person's feelings. They'd like to say something to make the other person laugh. Under pressure, however, many lose their sense of humor. They don't want to come across as sarcastic. They want to be firm, honest, and direct.

Don't be afraid to state your intentions early in a relationship. Set limits. For example, "It's fun going out with you, but I'm not into any physical stuff," or "Please don't do that. It makes me uncomfortable." Both convey what you want

Using drugs or drinking alcohol can cause you to lose control over your actions, which can make it more difficult to uphold your decision to abstain from sex.

without offending the other person. Each is a clear message about what you want.

Whatever you do, *don't* lead another person on. Don't act as if you want to get physical when you don't. And if the other person wants to stop, respect that, and stop. The other person is probably struggling with the same complicated issues as you.

Remember: Most teens don't plan to have sexual intercourse. It just happens. If you want to be sure it doesn't just happen to you, be prepared.

How do you say no when pressure is intense? One way is to be ready for any situation. Practice some of these responses to another person's come-on lines. You can use these or make up some of your own. Then you'll never find yourself at a loss for words.

Line: "If you really loved me, you'd do it."

Response: "I do love you. That's why I don't want to mess up our future together."

Line: "What's wrong with you? Don't you like men?"

Response: "Yes. But I know what I want, and for now, it's not this."

Line: "I'd love to have your baby."

Response: "You're a sweetheart, but I'm too young to be a father."

Line: "You're my one and only."

Response: "Good. Then there's no hurry for sex."

Line: "You're still a virgin?"

Response: "For sure. And proud of it."

Line: "Don't worry. I'm not old enough to be a parent."

Response: "If you're old enough to have sex, you may become a parent whether you like it or not."

Line: "Abstinence is no fun."

Response: "Neither is being pregnant for nine months."

Work on Your Self-Esteem

Self-esteem means feeling good about yourself. If you have high self-esteem, you will make good decisions for yourself—most of the time. If you make good decisions most of the time, you will begin to feel better and better about yourself.

To some people high self-esteem seems to come naturally. Take a look at the people you know. Some succeed in spite of tough lives. They take charge of themselves and make good choices. They feel confident about their direction in life. They are survivors.

On the other hand, we all know people who go through life without trying to improve themselves. They expect good things to happen to them with no effort on their part. Or they choose black clouds to walk under. They expect bad things to happen. They allow themselves to crash and burn. They act like victims. If you're 15, for example, you can't do anything about what happened to you when you were four. But you *can* do something about your life right now. If your self-esteem is low, how can you raise it? Here are some ideas:

Take a good look at yourself. Most people look in the mirror at least once a day. In addition, look *inside* yourself. Are you measuring up to your own standards? Learn to please yourself. Remember that you are your own best friend.

Take care of yourself. Treat yourself as if you already believe in yourself. Try giving up "crutches" such as cigarettes, alcohol, overeating, collecting lots of material goods, or sexual addictions. These unhealthy habits make you feel numb. They may temporarily wipe out uncomfortable feelings. But the relief lasts only for a short time. Soon the unnatural high wears off. A low period follows. Then to make yourself feel better, you may repeat the cycle. Finding out that you can live an even better life without "crutches" will do wonders for your self-esteem.

Set goals. Goal-setting is another way to raise your self-esteem. It is very satisfying to aim at a goal and then to achieve it. Try dividing your goals into short-term and long-term. A short-term goal might be to study 30 minutes every night or to turn in every assignment on time this week. A long-term goal might be to get into college. Don't just *set* the goals, but work toward achieving them. One at a time or two at a time. Some goals will be hard to reach. Try as hard as you can. Sometimes you will fail. That's okay. Try again. Give yourself credit for your efforts. Sometimes you will succeed.

Choose friends with high self-esteem. Hanging out with friends is very important to most young people. Peer pressure is strong. If you can raise your own self-esteem, you will be more likely to find friends with high self-esteem. If abstinence is your goal, find people who feel the same way.

Don't just stand there. Do something! Find important or fun things to do by yourself, with a date, or with friends. Remember: Sex isn't the only fun thing in the world. How about listening to your favorite music, watching a sunset, or walking barefoot in the grass? Add to that almost any kind of exercise. An hour of swimming, running, basketball, or tennis will give you a different kind of high. Take a hike, go dancing, or pump iron.

Will and Joe

Will: "I feel horny all the time."
Joe: "That's normal."
Will: "Sure. But what can I do about it?"
Joe: "Shoot baskets."
Will: "What?"
Joe: "Exercise. Jump rope. Lift weights. Jog. Play soccer. Volleyball. Do something.
Will: "Will it help?"
Joe: "Yeah. Exercise reduces tension. Takes the edge off."
Will: "I don't want to ruin my sex drive. I just want to control it."
Joe: "Exercise helps. It also makes you feel better about yourself."

Get a job. Your interests don't *have* to include burning calories or building muscles. Most people have a creative side. Do you like to draw, write, sculpt, or make jewelry? Some teens (even pre-teens) have turned their creative interest into a business. Fifteen-year-old Brian airbrushes designs on T-shirts. Kylie and Kelly, both 12, make cards and bookmarks. Greg and Ken, 13, cover graffiti on houses and garage doors with their paint and brushes. Latasha, 14, bakes and sells candy and cookies. Melissa is only 11, but she earns money making maps and floor plans on her computer. Your can also mow lawns, baby-sit, or deliver newspapers.

Volunteer. If you find yourself with time on your hands and don't have a job, volunteer. Help someone who needs your help. Most towns have at least one nursing home. Big cities may have hundreds of them. Find one close to your house. Many older people are lonely and would love to talk or play cards. Animal shelters usually need volunteers.

Write in a journal. If you like writing, buy yourself a blank book. Every night before you go to sleep, write in your journal: things you like about yourself, things others like about you, things you did today that made you feel good about yourself. Resist the urge to compare yourself to anyone else.

All of the above are ways to increase your self-esteem. That doesn't mean you won't have bad days or self-doubts. But you will be a happier person, involved in life. You'll probably be able to see more of the "big picture." There's more to life than sex.

Still, people *are* sexual beings. In spite of high self-esteem and many activities, sex may be on your mind a lot. That's okay. You may find it best to leave it there for now.

Just Say No?

Sometimes it's not easy to "just say no." If you're not sure where you stand on the subject of abstinence, stop and ask yourself three questions right now.

What are my sexual choices?

What are the possible consequences of each choice?

How will these consequences affect my short-term future or my long-term future?

Consider a scenario. On your third date, your date wants to have sex. You resist for a while because sex before marriage is against your values. Finally, though, you give in because you are afraid he or she will leave you if you continue to resist. You're not completely certain how you feel about having had sex, but you're glad that you did it for the sake of the relationship. But then one of your friends sees your partner out with someone else. He or she doesn't call very often anymore. You feel betrayed. Besides that, you've lost your self-respect, and you're angry that you let yourself down. However, you can regain your self-respect by forgiving yourself, admitting you made

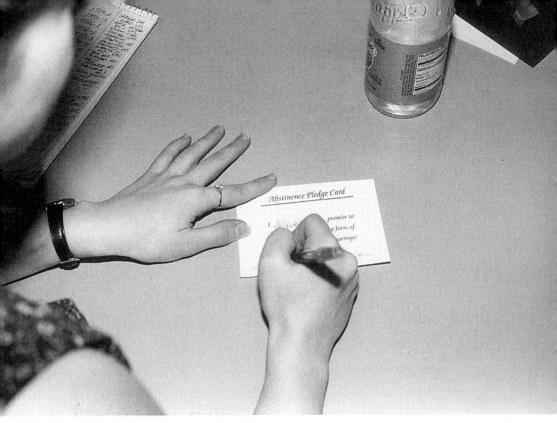

Signing an abstinence pledge card can help you stick to your goal of abstaining from sex until marriage.

a mistake, and making different choices the next time.

Make a Pledge of Abstinence

If you have decided that abstinence is for you, you might want to "go public" with your goal. Signing a pledge card is one way some people let the world know their plan. They announce that they will remain celibate until marriage. Many church-sponsored groups make these cards available. If you pledge abstinence with a group, you will have the support of others like yourself. What if you can't find such a group? Then make your own pledge card. Write out something like this. Sign it and carry it in your wallet.

"I, Jim Johnson (or Jane Jones), pledge to be sexually abstinent from now until the day I marry. I realize this decision will protect me, my partners (especially my future mate), any children I may have, and the rest of my family."

Masturbation (Self-Pleasuring, Self-Gratification)

For centuries the "M" word has been a bad word in many circles. People did it and still do it, but nobody wants to talk about it. Some people think masturbation is bad. Some churches condemn it. One survey found that half of American adults consider it a no-no.

But medical experts say there is nothing wrong with masturbation and that there is a lot that is right about it. It reduces sexual tensions and stress, it does not give anyone AIDS or STD, and it does not cause pregnancy. The term "outercourse" describes masturbation with a partner.

Abstinence is defined as not participating in sexual intercourse until marriage. Abstinence *may* mean you don't do romantic kissing, necking, petting, masturbation, or outercourse. *Your* version of abstinence is your decision.

Glossary—*Explaining New Words*

abstinence Postponing of sex. Also called celibacy, chastity, or "not going all the way."

acne Pimples, zits.

AIDS Acquired immunodeficiency syndrome, a fatal disease contracted by sexual intercourse with an infected person, by infected blood products, or by sharing of unsterilized needles by IV drug users.

addiction Repetitive compulsive behavior.

bisexual A person sexually attracted to both males and females.

cervix Opening to the uterus.

chlamydia Most common sexually transmitted disease. If untreated, it can cause sterility and other serious symptoms.

clitoris Sex organ that becomes sexually excited.

contagious Able to be passed to someone else; catching.

douche To rinse out the vagina with a liquid.

ejaculate In the male, having an orgasm.

emotional intimacy Emotional closeness.

erection Hardening of the penis under arousal.

fallopian tubes Connection between top of uterus and ovaries.

hormones Chemical substances in the blood that influence body functioning.

genitals Sex organs.

gonorrhea Sexually transmitted disease spread by direct contact. Untreated, it can cause sterility.

herpes Sexually transmitted disease caused by a virus. Painful attacks come and go.

heterosexual A person attracted to those of the opposite sex.

immune system Organs and substances in the blood that fight infection.

infatuation Superficial love.

infertility Difficulty in getting pregnant.

labia majora Large "lips" in female genital area.

labia minora Small "lips" in female genital area.

lesbian Woman sexually attracted to other women.

masturbation Sexual self-pleasuring.

menstruation Discharge that occurs each month when the uterus sheds its lining.

nocturnal emissions Male ejaculations during sleep. Also called "wet dreams."

outercourse Mutual masturbation.

ovaries The two female internal organs that store eggs.

penis Male external genital organ.

petting Sexually touching another person.

pregnancy   Nine-month developmental period of infant inside maternal uterus.

puberty   Beginning of hormonal and sexual changes in males and females.

reflex   An automatic body response.

scrotum   Male external genital organ containing testicles.

self-esteem   Feeling good about oneself.

syphilis   Sexually transmitted disease caused by bacteria. Untreated, can cause death.

semen   Milky fluid that comes out of penis during orgasm.

sperm   Tiny moving organism in male semen.

sterility   Inability to have children.

testicles   Male sex organs inside scrotum.

vagina   Female genital organ extending from the uterus to the labia minora.

uterus   Pear-shaped organ in which baby grows. Sometimes called "womb."

vulva   Genital area of females.

Where to Get Help

Hotlines
IN THE U.S.:
Centers for Disease Control and Prevention
National STD Hotline (800) 277-8922
National AIDS Hotline:

    English-speaking   (800) 342-2437
    En Español   (800) 344-7432
    Hearing Impaired   (800) 243-7889
    Planned Parenthood (800) 472-7162

IN CANADA:
STD and AIDS Hotline (Winnipeg) (800) 782-2437

Organizations
IN THE U.S.:
Athletes for Abstinence
A. C. Green Programs for Youth
P.O. Box 17283
Los Angeles, CA 90017
(800) ACA-YOUTH
(800) 222-9688

Planned Parenthood Federation of America
810 Seventh Avenue.
New York, NY 10019
(212) 541-7800

Sex Information and Education Council of the
  United States (SIECUS)
130 West 42nd Street
New York, NY 10036
(212) 819-9770

IN CANADA:
Planned Parenthood Federation of Canada
1 Nicholas Street, Suite 430
Ottawa, Ontario K1N 7B7
(613) 238-4474

Canadian Public Health Association
National AIDS Clearinghouse
1565 Carling Ave., Suite 400
Ottawa, Ontario K1Z 8R1
(613) 725-3769

Health Canada, Publications Division
(613) 952-9191
AIDS Yukon Alliance
(403) 663-2437

For Further Reading

Brown, Gabrielle. *The New Celibacy*. New York:
McGraw-Hill Book Company, 1980.

Kolodny, Nancy; Kolodny, Robert; and Bratter,
Thomas. *Smart Choices*. Boston: Little Brown
and Company, 1986.

McKay, Matthew, and Fanning, Patrick. *Self-
Esteem*. Oakland, CA: New Harbinger
Publications, 1987.

Rench, Janice E. *Teen Sexuality: Decisions and
Choices*. Minneapolis: Lerner Publications
Company, 1988.

Sawyer, Kieran. *Sex and the Teenager: Choices and
Decisions*. Notre Dame, IN: Ave Maria Press,
1990.

Index

A
abortion, 19
acne, 21
activity, sexual, 11
AIDS (acquired
    immunodeficiency
    syndrome), 10, 30, 34,
    42–43, 45, 46
alcohol, 45
anal intercourse, 34
Athletes for Abstinence (AFA),
    34

B
birth control, 30
bisexual, 32
body odor, 21
breast growth, 17

C
chlamydia, 43
choices, sexual, 7, 9, 11–13, 36,
    37–38
clitoris, 16
communication, 38, 45
condom, 10, 43

E
eggs, 16
erection, uncontrolled, 21
exercise, 52

F
fallopian tubes, 16
feelings, sexual, 9–10, 33–34
fulfillment, sex as, 11–13

G
gay, 32, 33

goals, setting, 51
gonorrhea, 43
Green, A. C., 34
Green, Darrell, 34
growth spurt, 17, 19

H
hair, body, 21
herpes, 43
heterosexual, 32
HIV (human immunodeficiency
    virus), 42–43
homosexual, 32, 33
hormones, 8, 17, 19

I
infatuation, 27
infertility, 42
intimacy
    emotional, 28
    physical, 28, 31

J
job, getting, 52–53
journal, keeping, 53

L
labia majora/minora, 16
lesbian, 32
limits, setting, 47
love and sex, 26–27

M
masturbation, 56
menstrual periods, 17–18, 21

N
Non-Touchers, 23
no, saying, 47–56

O

orgasm, 14, 16
outercourse, 56
ovaries, 16

P

penis, 14, 19
petting, 23, 24
pregnancy, 10, 14, 16, 18, 19,
    21, 30, 36, 40, 43–44, 45
pressure, 11, 38, 46, 47, 48
puberty, 17, 21

Q

questions
    about homosexuality, 31–32
    about love and sex, 27–31

R

relationships, 8, 13
    changed by sex, 30, 45
    committed, 31
    homosexual, 34
    responsibilities of, 25–27, 30,
        36, 46
    sex as part of, 28–29, 30
respect
    for friends and family,
        37–40
    for partner, 38
    self-, 13, 36, 46
    for your children, 38–39
Robinson, David, 34

S

scrotum, 14, 19
self-esteem, 27, 32–33, 49–53
semen, 19
sex
    premarital, 38
    safer, 26, 43
sexual abstinence, 13, 19,
    22–36, 36–46
    choosing, 45
    pledge of, 55–56
sexual intercourse, 10, 14,
    22–23, 42, 48
sexual organs, 8, 14, 16, 17
sperm, 14, 19
STDS (sexually transmitted
    diseases), 10, 30, 34, 36,
    38, 40–42, 45, 46
sterility, 42
syphilis, 43

T

testicles, 14
Touchers, 24

U

uterus, 16, 18

V

vagina, 14, 16
volunteering, 53

W

wet dreams, 21

About the Author

Barbara Moe is a mother, a nurse, a social worker, and a writer. She loves working with young people and helping them face challenges.

Photo Credits

Cover by Michael Brandt; p. 2 by Katherine Hsu; p. 29 by Yung-Hee Chia; p. 37 by Marcus Schaffer; all other photos by Kim Sonsky.